ONE

Don't get me wrong. It's not that life is really BAD on Capella-4G. It's one of Earth's oldest colonies, not some backwater mud ball. And it has one of the busiest spaceports in the sector. A hundred ships go in and out every three days.

And that's part of the problem, from my front porch, I can see those ships climbing toward the heavens. Even with the muting fields, I am sometimes sure I can hear the thunder of their engines. Like something in a dream.

Dreamer. Yes, that what Mom calls me. Head in the stars. Always looking up.

It's in my blood, I tell her. My father — her husband — died out there in the cold deeps of space. He was a pilot on a freighter, and it was attacked by Looters. When that happens, the only option is to abandon ship and hope the SafeSuits will keep you alive until rescue arrives. If it arrives. I've heard of one guy who was in his SafeSuit for three years! Can you imagine? Drifting between the stars, alone.

But I need to tell you my story in the right order. I need to pick a starting point. And this is as good as any, the day Mom sent me and 262 on the weekly run into City Nine for supplies. It's always hardest when I have to go into the City.

DREAMER

TWO

The market is just a few miles from the spaceport. There, the ground rumbles when the bigger ships take off. And there the air is full of alien sounds and scents. Plenty of humans, sure. This is an Earth colony, like I said. But lots and lots of out-worlders.

Today, I wasn't paying them much notice, though. I wandered through the stalls with 262, but my mind wasn't on the collecting of supplies. My mind was where Mom says it always is — in the stars.

One of the big haulers took off while we were at market. It shot up faster than anything that size has any business moving, balancing on a sword of fire and smoke. It was out of sight in a couple of heart beats, but in my mind's eye I could still see it climbing, as the sky changed to black, and the stars came out even though it was only just past noon.

Like from somewhere far, far off, I heard 262 speaking to me. "Miss Eliza. Are you listening? It's time to head home."

"I'm listening." I wasn't. But I fell in step with the old family retainer — how old? Half a dozen generations of us he'd served — and we made our way back to where I'd left the UniBike.

MARKET

THREE

I said it was hardest when I had to go into the City, but this time of day was hard, too. Around dinner time, when the sky darkens and the stars come out.

The other moons are always in the sky, of course. Dozens of them, swinging in their big, lazy orbits around Capella-Four. But it's the stars that make my heart ache. Sometimes I feel like my heart is going to just lift me up, carry me away from the porch, the house, the grumblings of the shoo-cows as they jostle each other at the toughs.

Yeah, pick me up and carry me far above the clouds, to feel the air grow thin and cold, and see the stars grow bright as shattered diamonds. Sharp and steady, beyond the atmosphere. No twinkling. Like constant beacons to guide the ships across the spacelanes.

"Honey, time to wash up!"

Mom. The whirr of her salad mixer is so mundane. Everything is mundane. Ordinary. Only the stars are special.

"Ellie's dreaming again," says Seth, my baby brother. He was born while our father was on that last freighter flight. He has no memories of him, not like I do. Doesn't miss him.

"Shuddup, spud," I say, and head inside to the necessary. And in that moment, for some reason, my mind is made up.

FAMILY

FOUR

It's past curfew for someone my age — fifteen in three months — so I know there's all kinds of trouble I could get into if a pol-car stops my UniBike. And they can do that with a flip of a switch.

So I try not to bring extra attention to myself. I cruise through the sea of shifting lights, weaving between the big haulers, dodging the privates. I stay safely under the speed limit, even though that means taking almost an hour to get where I'm going, even after I pass the city limits.

City Nine. Like the name says, it was the ninth city started on this colony world. Almost three hundred years ago, when this planet was still wild and raw, like the worlds I dream of.

A hauler blasts his horn at me. I've been daydreaming again. I need to concentrate on where I'm going. Only a few minutes now.

Still, I can't help wondering how Mom will react she when she finds my note. I kept it simple. "I've got to go. I wouldn't be my father's daughter if I didn't. I promise to let you know where I am as soon as I know myself. I love you all. Eliza."

My full name. Being formal. Trying to make this seem like something serious. Something grown up. Not just a crazy kid off on an even crazier adventure. I known 262 will go out of his mechanical mind. He was programmed to take care of me. I feel bad about that.

RUNAWAY

FIVE

The spaceport. Like I said, this is one of the busiest in the sector. Maybe a hundred ships come and go every day. Big ships, small ships. Commercial, private, other.

It's the "other" that interests me.

A lot of unlicensed freighters come through this port. They land empty and take off full, and all the port authorities look the other way the whole time. It's like that on a thousand worlds. Business is business.

My Dad was on a commercial ship, properly licensed, so I'm not really sure what he'd think about me specifically looking for a "rogue." He wouldn't approve, I'm sure, but he'd probably also applaud my moxie. After all, if I'm going to take this chance, I might as well take it big!

On the edge of the port, I swing the UniBike into a parking stall and let down the inflation on the wheel. It settles lower to the ground, almost like its sleeping. I dismount, and wonder if I will ever see it again. If it stays here more than a few days — and it will, if I am successful — it will be impounded or stolen.

I grab my gear off the back of the saddle and look around for the best way to get into the port. Even at this time of night the traffic is heavy. That's why I chose this gate. The security scans will have a lot of vehicles to keep track of. They're not likely to notice one small human slipping by.

They don't.

I get past the gate and duck around the first block of buildings. I find the narrow passageways, the alleys, the service corridors. I slip deep into the port, and pretty soon I am ducking and weaving my way across the landing field.

There are maybe three dozen ships prepping. And one of them is just what I'm looking for. A big freighter with no markings. There's a swirl and buzz of crew all around it. Big pallets of random cargo being lifted and loaded. The crew are either not bothering to check the crates individually, or that's already been done.

I scurry around the piles of crates, feeling like a mouse hiding from a cat. I check maybe forty locks before I find one that's loose. I give it an extra tug and it pops. The cargo is condensed food packets, and the crate is only about two thirds full.

I climb in and wait — and not for long. There's a thump and a jerk, and a feeling of vertigo as the crate I'm in is lifted onto a pallet and then up into the cargo bay. We roll for a bit and then stop with a thump.

I hear alarms, muted by the walls of the crate. I think for a moment maybe I've been found out. Then the whole world punches me in the back.

STOWAWAY

SEVEN

This is the part of my plan that's not best thought through. In the rest of the ship, there will be acceleration couches to cushion the crew against the rush of the launch. I don't have one of those in my crate. I settle back on the food packs and try to stay conscious.

I think I manage it. It's dark in the crate, so I'm not sure if I black out. If I do, it's just as black when I wake up.

Then there's a shift. I tumble about inside the crate as up becomes sideways, and then settles for being down. The ship has left planetary gravity, and the artificial gravity plates are purring up to power. Slowly, I feel my forty kilos settle back to something like itself. The food packs stop dancing and lie still under me.

Now, the next part of my unplanned plan: what do I do about getting out of this crate and finding my way around the ship? As far as I can tell, no other cargo has been loaded on top of me. I put the side of my head against the inside wall of the crate and listen. I can hear muffled sounds, work sounds. Some of the other crates must have come loose during launch. I can hear crew shouting as they push them back where they're supposed to be.

I listen to the sounds of movement. The thud of boots on the metal decks. The noise is dying down. Probably the loading is considered finished, and there'll be no one down here until we reach wherever we're going.

At least, that's what I think.

LAUNCH

EIGHT

It's not the ugliest face I've ever seen, but it's in the top ten. It looms over me suddenly, as the lid of my crate is yanked back. A three-fingered paw grabs me, and the face yells. It's like air being let out of a toy balloon, a blubbering shriek.

"I don't think it understands you," a more human-looking crewman chuckles. The big alien tightens his grip and hauls me out of the crate.

"Where did you come from?" The alien's voice is soft and almost melodious when it's not yelling. It's tiny eyes open wider, and they're almost kind.

"Capella-4G," I say.

"Figures," says the other crewman. "She came on at the last stop. She couldn't have been here much longer than that without being found."

The alien makes more noises like a deflating balloon, but softer this time.

"Oh, no!" says the human. "You take her to the bridge, *****!" He makes a sound like someone blowing a raspberry. I realize it must be the alien's name. "I got better things to do than spend the rest of the trip babysitting!"

I start to ask what that means, but Raspberry is already pulling me toward a exit portal.

"The Captain is going to want a few hundred words with you," the aliens says, in English again. The small eyes turn in my direction and narrow again. "I would not want to be in your boots!"

Through the deep corridors of the ship we go. Everything is close and packed tight. Not a cubic centimeter of wasted space, as crew members squeeze past each other. Sometimes it seems like there's no room for Raspberry to go any further, but somehow he makes it through even the most narrow spaces, hauling and pushing me along.

And then, suddenly, it all opens out, and we're on the Bridge. The spaces are wide and high, and through the view dome at the front I see the Capella system gliding past.

Humans and aliens of many species are busy at the controls. I spot a few robots, too. But in all that, two figures stand out, a man and a woman.

"What in blazes do you have there, *****," she asks. Her tone is so cold there is suddenly nothing comical about my captor's name.

"Human female," Raspberry says. "Found her in the cargo hold."

When he speaks, the Captain's voice is like a rumble from somewhere deep in the ship. "A stowaway?" He steps forward to examine me up close. "What's your name, brat?"

"Eliza Smith," I say.

He looks at me through narrowed eyes. "There was a time when captains were authorized to throw stowaways off their ships," he says. "Most chose to go without a SafeSuit."

The woman smiles, but it's not friendly. "Lucky for you we don't do that any more."

BRIDGE

TEN

"She'll need to be fitted," says the Captain. "She can't wander around the ship in civvies."

"She can't wander at all," says the woman, who I've decided is the First Mate. "*****, you found her, you're in charge of her. I think one of my spare suits may fit."

Raspberry takes hold of me again, and drags me off the Bridge. Now I understand what that first human crewman meant about "babysitting." Over the next few days, Raspberry does not let me wander anywhere without close observation.

I get fitted for a SafeSuit. "Fitted" is generous. The suit adjusts, like they're made to, but the First Mate is taller than me, and some of the joints bite when I bend. Still, this walking spaceship is the only thing that stands between me and a nasty death if the hull is breached.

Which it is.

My ninth day aboard. I've been assigned down to the engineering section, where I'm given busywork "To keep you out of trouble." But trouble comes looking for me — for all of us.

Without any warning the hull explodes inward. The blast is followed by echoes from all parts of the ship. We're under attack!

"Looters," shouts Raspberry, grabbing for me as the air rushes out of the gaping hole in the hull. My helmet snaps closed automatically as everything turns upside down. Being caught in the heart of a tornado would be a pleasure ride compared to this!

ATTACK

ELEVEN

We're sucked right out of the ship. All around us there are explosions and darting Looter ships. I get only a brief glimpse as the closest planet looms up.

Raspberry is still hanging onto me. I realize small jets are firing in the SafeSuits. We're being guided automatically away from the attacking Looters and toward the safety of the planet. At least, I hope it will be safe!

If I thought the madness of being sucked out of the ship was bad, it was nothing compared to this! The SafeSuits protect us from the physical effects of plunging through a planet's atmosphere, but there's nothing they can do about what I see and hear.

I see other members of the crew making similar plunges. Like I said, when the Looters attack, the only option is to abandon ship. The part of my brain that isn't entirely occupied by wanting to scream and thrash wonders how many will survive — and how close together we'll all land.

If we land. It's not a given. SafeSuits were created to be as good as spaceships, but they have their limits. The manufacturers admit they work best as lifeboats, keeping people alive as they drift through space. They're not really meant as re-entry vehicles.

But Raspberry never lets go. I guess you might say we have become something like friends in the time I've been in his charge. There was no reason to grab me, after all. But obviously Raspberry wanted to be sure I got clear safely. And I can tell this ride would have been even rougher without those big arms wrapped around me.

PLUNGE

TWELVE

The landing is less than graceful. About a mile up, the SafeSuit deploys a parachute, and slows our descent to something more reasonable.

But the planet seems to be mostly jungle, and we hit the canopy at a bad angle. The parachute tangles and Raspberry's grip on me is broken. I tumble through the thick leaves and branches like — well, like just what I am, a helpless human in a couple hundred kilos of suit.

Internal systems keep the fall from shaking me to mush, and the ground is soft when it catches me. Mostly it seems to be vegetable matter. The solid ground is buried under layer upon layer of plants.

Sensing a clean atmosphere, the suit peels back my helmet, and the scents and sounds of the planet flood over me. It's a sickening concoction. Life and death mingled together, and all around shrieks and howls from unseen creatures who have been disturbed by our arrival.

Suddenly, one of those creatures is in front of me. I have a momentary impression of something like a bald monkey with big fangs, and then it's leaping for me. I try to dodge and fall over backward.

Then the jungle floor bursts into a bright flash. Still tangled in the parachute harness, I see Raspberry firing a warning blast in front of the monkey.

It takes the hint and scampers into the concealing growth around me.

JUNGLE

THIRTEEN

Raspberry gets loose of the tangled harness and drops down to the ground beside me. Snuffling sounds emerge from those constantly writhing tentacles.

"Standard survival drill." Raspberry's tone is very professional.

"I don't know what that is," I say, somewhat sheepishly.

Raspberry shows me how to strip down the SafeSuit, opening compartments to deploy equipment and carrying cases. Pretty soon we're down to our most basic equipment and clothing.

"Which way do we go?" I ask.

Raspberry considers. "I think I saw Captain Harris and Exec Soo falling to the north of us. Best we head that way."

So we do.

It's a hard trek. Every square inch of the jungle floor seems determined to trip and entangle us. The communicator Raspberry carries crackles and pops, but there's no incoming signal. Raspberry says it may be damaged, or it may be something in the electromagnetic fields of this planet.

"Do we even know which planet?" I ask.

Raspberry says no. Before the Looters attack we were on course, but Raspberry wasn't paying any attention to where we were. I was the main focus of attention.

I grumble a bit about having the blame dumped on me, but I'm not unhappy for long. The jungle thins out a bit and we step into a small clearing. A stream cuts through the middle of it, and odd-looking fish leap from its waters.

But it's the other side of the stream that brings the best news.

REUNION

FOURTEEN

Captain Harris takes immediate command of our little party, and Raspberry is clearly happy to let him do so. Exec Soo says she had determined there is something in the makeup of these trees and plants that is messing with our transmitters, but Harris says he got a fix on some open land about twenty kilometers to the west.

We head that way, as the day grows hotter and the air gets thicker and harder to breathe. All our energies are focused on crossing the tangling floor, and finding the easiest path through the trees. Maybe that's why none of us notice we are no longer alone.

We'll get a better look at these natives later. They're a bit smaller than an average human, shaped for moving quickly through the jungle canopy. They communicate is clicks and whistles that blend into the noises all around, giving no indication of them being right above us.

And that's where they stay, as we trudge along. Moving quickly and easily, with only a fraction of the effort we're using, they hop from branch to branch, not letting us out of their sight, but also not taking any hostile moves against us.

It goes like that for about ten hours. Then we start to notice that the jungle is thinning, and the animal noises are growing quiet. Luckily, that tips Captain Harris that all is not as it should be. We slow almost to a crawl as we approach the clearing he spotted from the air.

FIFTEEN

Now we see why the jungle noises have died down. A Looter ship has landed in the clearing. Several of the crew have disembarked.

This is my first time seeing Looters in person. Most of the imagery we have of them is from scraps of video captured by people fleeing their attacks. They're bigger than I imagined, and their own versions of SafeSuits make them look almost robotic.

Captain Harris draws his gun as we move into defensive positions. I'm wondering how effective it will be against the Looter suits. I start to ask Raspberry, but I'm motioned to silence.

We crouch there for ten or fifteen minutes, until my knees start to ache. I want to shift, but I'm afraid the rustle of the ground cover might give us away.

The Looters wander without any real purpose. From what little I have learned of them, I guess they've probably sunk a shaft into the ground beneath their ship and are sucking up elements to refuel. I wonder if there are any more of them, scattered around the planet.

All at once, the Looter closest to us stops. He turns in our direction, raising his rifle. My stomach shrinks to the size of a grape, and it's all I can do to keep myself from running.

Captain Harris shifts, raising his gun and drawing a bead on the closest Looter. If this is where it ends, we're not going to go down without a fight.

But it turns out it's not us the Looter is interested in.

SIXTEEN

All three Looters open fire at once, but they're aiming above us, into the canopy.

Right then is when we learn the natives have been following us. They shriek and scream as the Looter's blasts slice through them. They rain down all around us.

It's the first time I've seen death on this scale. Maybe a dozen of the natives come crashing down. Some of them are not clean kills. They writhe and squeal. It's painful to see and hear.

Captain Harris and Exec Soo don't do anything. I understand that they don't want to give us away, but I want to yell at them to help. The natives clearly don't understand what's happening to them. They scatter, but the Looters keep raking the canopy with their blasters.

Even back beyond my sight, deep in the heavy leaves and branches I can hear the screams. It seems like there is nowhere the natives can go that the Looters cannot reach them.

Something like laughter is issuing from the Looter's suits. They can see as well as I can that the natives are intelligent, but they don't care. They're shooting for sport.

And I can't take it any more.

SEVENTEEN

It's maybe the dumbest thing I have ever done in my not-so-very-long life, but I grab Raspberry's blaster and start shooting.

To my great surprise, the Looter nearest to me goes down easy. The blaster slices through him (?) like a hot blade through janna melon. Something very much like a scream issues from the suit, and is cut short. I catch a brief whiff like bad barbecue, and then everyone is yelling.

Raspberry grabs me and pulls me down below the top of our log cover. We scurry to the left on all fours, no pretense of grace or dignity. We just need to move!

IMPULSE

EIGHTEEN

It's lucky that we do. One of the other Looters opens fire on our last location, and everything the beam hits turns to burning ash. Trees, rocks, leaves. Even the bodies of the fallen natives. Gone in a heartbeat.

And that could have been us!

"Keep moving!" Captain Harris shouts over the screech of the Looter's weapon "Keep moving!"

Suddenly the other Looter's are firing, too. Surely they must know the area the first one scorched can't possibly have any life in it? But, they don't care, do they? Once again, they're shooting for sport. For fun.

RETALIATION

NINETEEN

Suddenly, the sounds of the weapons change. Not a screech any more. Something more like a low hum. I feel it before I hear it. It rattles my teeth and turns my joints to jelly.

"Keep… going…" says Soo, but she can barely get the words out.

Captain Harris stumbles and falls. Soo goes next. I keep clawing at the undergrowth, trying to drag myself along, but the air is turning to concrete around me. I'm swimming through tar.

There's a big thump behind me, and Raspberry is down.

Almost with half a brain, I realize I am too. Not unconscious, not dead. But down, unable to move. Barely able to think. I hear the chatter between the Looters. Grunting, animal sounds. There's enough working in my brain to wonder if that's really how they sound, of if that's the best I can do to hear them in my befuddled state.

And now I remember other things I have heard about the Looters. They don't just steal merchandise. They grab people. To trade as slaves.

CAPTURED

TWENTY

In my groggy state, what happens next seems to be at super speed. The natives are back, and they launch themselves into the Looters like arrows from a bow. They seem to know exactly where to strike. I get the feeling this is not the first time they have seen Looters on their planet.

I manage to push up on one arm for a better look, but in my stupor everything around me is a blur. I hear the cries of the natives, and the guttural screams of the Looters.

It's all over very quickly, both in my time and in real time. The Looters are down. The natives dance their victory, crowing over the fallen Looters.

Then they turn to us. I figure this is the end, but they don't attack. They gather us up — it takes eight of them to shift Raspberry — and pretty soon we're being transported to their village.

Over the next few hours, the numbness of the Looter weapon begins to wear off. We can talk again. We can move — though we look like drunk puppets.

Through a combinations of gestures and noises, we can communicate with the natives. Seems my shooting that Looter wasn't my dumbest move ever after all. That's what cued the natives that we were on their side.

ALLIES

TWENTY ONE

Soo gets her transmitter working, and we send a distress signal. It will take three days for it to reach any nearby ship, she guesses, and twice that for a rescue ship to arrive.

We settle down to get friendly with the natives. They feed us, and over the week or so that we're with them we manage to get them to understand what's going to happen.

So, they're real excited when the rescue ship arrives. I get the impression they've seen plenty of Looter ships, and that many of their people have been killed and taken. But now they will be under protection, and they like that idea.

Horns are blown and drums are pounded as the rescue ship drops out of the sky, light as a feather despite its huge size.

We say our fond farewells to the natives, and make the short trek to the ship. This is not its first landing on this planet, it seems. About seventy percent of our crew have been picked up, too.

We never do find out what happened to the rest.

It's too easy to guess.

RESCUE

TWENTY TWO

I get sorted out and processed. The orders are to ship me home. Nothing I can do about it. Raspberry gets all weepy, and I admit I shed a drop or two saying goodbye to the big guy.

I don't even see Harris and Soo before I'm parceled off to a cruiser headed in my direction. The whole thing takes about three weeks — most of it in hyperspace.

All in all, it seems like no time at all before the cops are dropping me at my door. Mom and Seth and 262 are so happy to see me. I expected to be grounded for life, but Mom's just relieved to see me home.

Mom signs some documents for the police, and all of a sudden it's like nothing happened. We sit down to dinner while 262 serves, and another day is another day.

That night, I lie in my bed and think about all that happened. A genuine adventure. Life and death! And becoming something like pals with an alien I'm not likely ever to see again. That makes me sad, for a while.

But the days roll on, and the chores pile up, and pretty soon I'm back to my old routine.

HOMECOMING

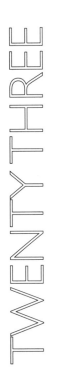

TWENTY THREE

Which includes standing on a hilltop overlooking the spaceport. Dreaming.

DREAMER

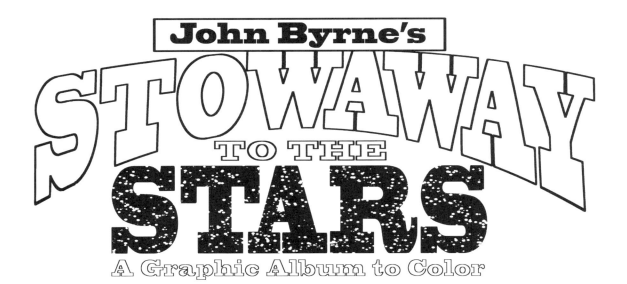

John Byrne's Stowaway to the Stars
A Graphic Album to Color

Art and Story by
JOHN BYRNE

Editor: Chris Ryall
Book Design: Robbie Robbins
Publisher Ted Adams

With Special Thanks to
SCOTT ADSIT
for knocking over the
first domino

For international rights,
please contact licensing@idwpublishing.com

ISBN: 978-1-63140-769-7

19 18 17 16   1 2 3 4

Ted Adams, CEO & Publisher
Greg Goldstein, President & COO
Robbie Robbins, EVP/Sr. Graphic Artist
Chris Ryall, Chief Creative Officer/Editor-in-Chief
Laurie Windrow, Senior Vice President of Sales & Marketing
Matthew Ruzicka, CPA, Chief Financial Officer
Dirk Wood, VP of Marketing
Lorelei Bunjes, VP of Digital Services
Jeff Webber, VP of Licensing, Digital and Subsidiary Rights
Jerry Bennington, VP of New Product Development

Facebook: facebook.com/idwpublishing
Twitter: @idwpublishing
YouTube: youtube.com/idwpublishing
Tumblr: tumblr.idwpublishing.com
Instagram: instagram.com/idwpublishing

JOHN BYRNE'S STOWAWAY TO THE STARS: A GRAPHIC ALBUM TO COLOR. NOVEMBER 2016. FIRST PRINTING. © John Byrne. © 2016 Idea and Design Works, LLC. All Rights Reserved. The IDW logo is registered in the U.S. Patent and Trademark Office. IDW Publishing, a division of Idea and Design Works, LLC. Editorial offices: 2765 Truxtun Road, San Diego, CA 92106. Any similarities to persons living or dead are purely coincidental. With the exception of artwork used for review purposes, none of the contents of this publication may be reprinted without the permission of Idea and Design Works, LLC. Printed in Korea.
IDW Publishing does not read or accept unsolicited submissions of ideas, stories, or artwork.